this book belongs to:

_____

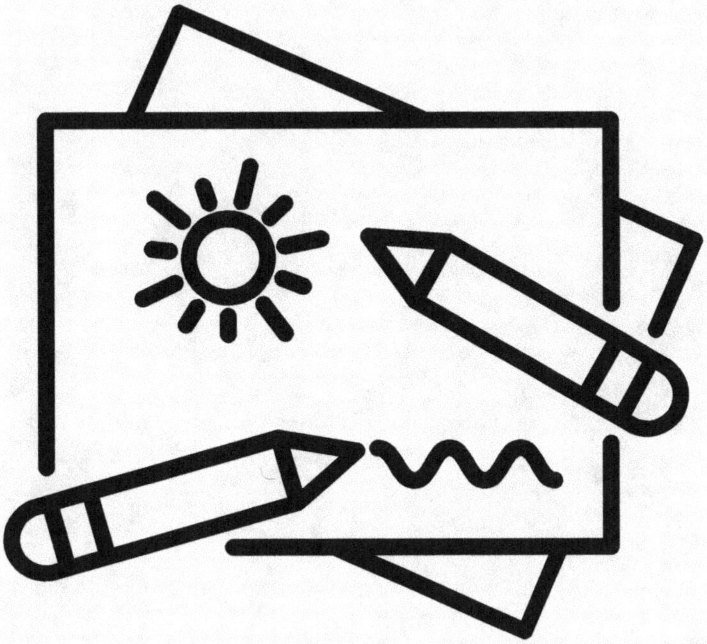

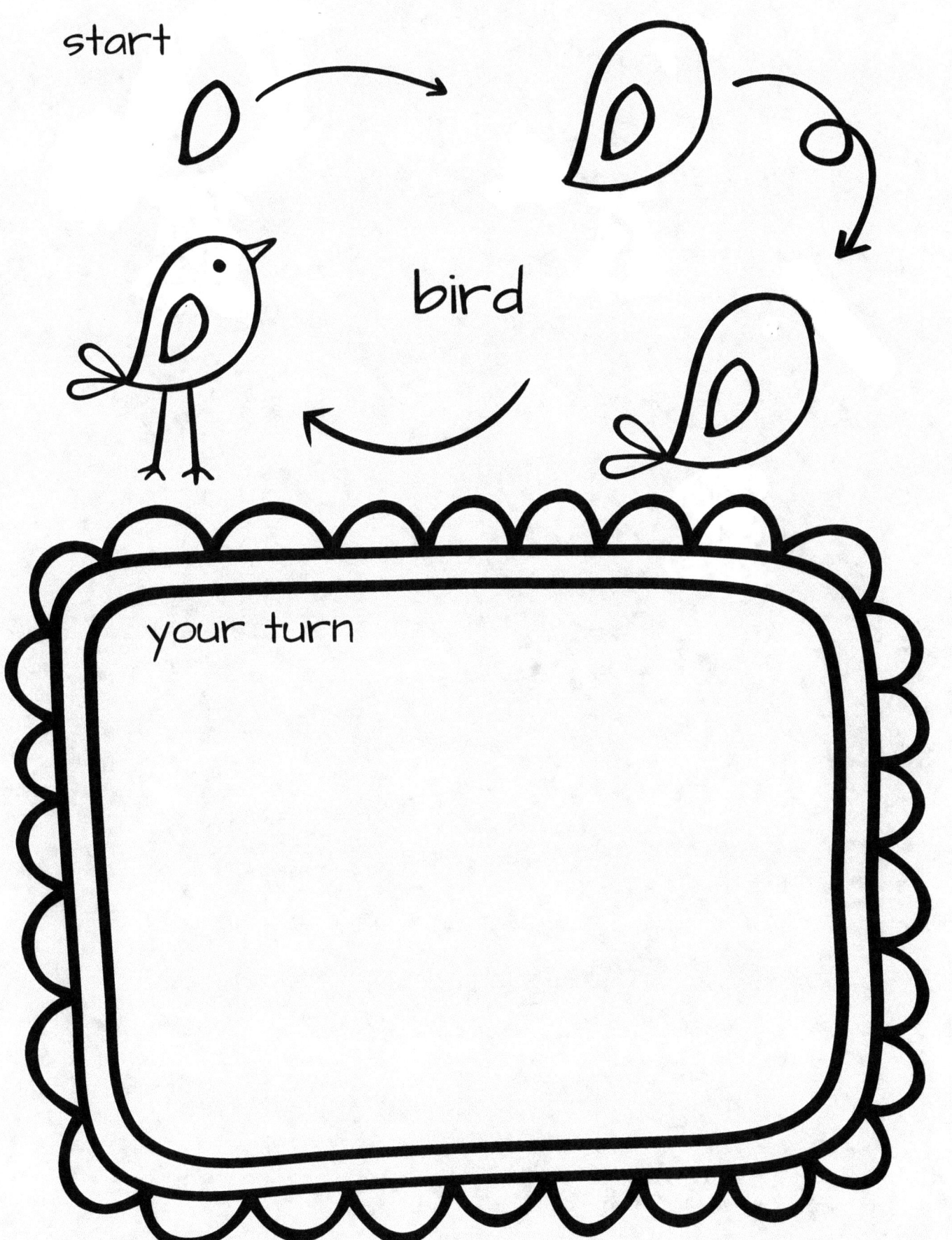

Try again and then color.

start

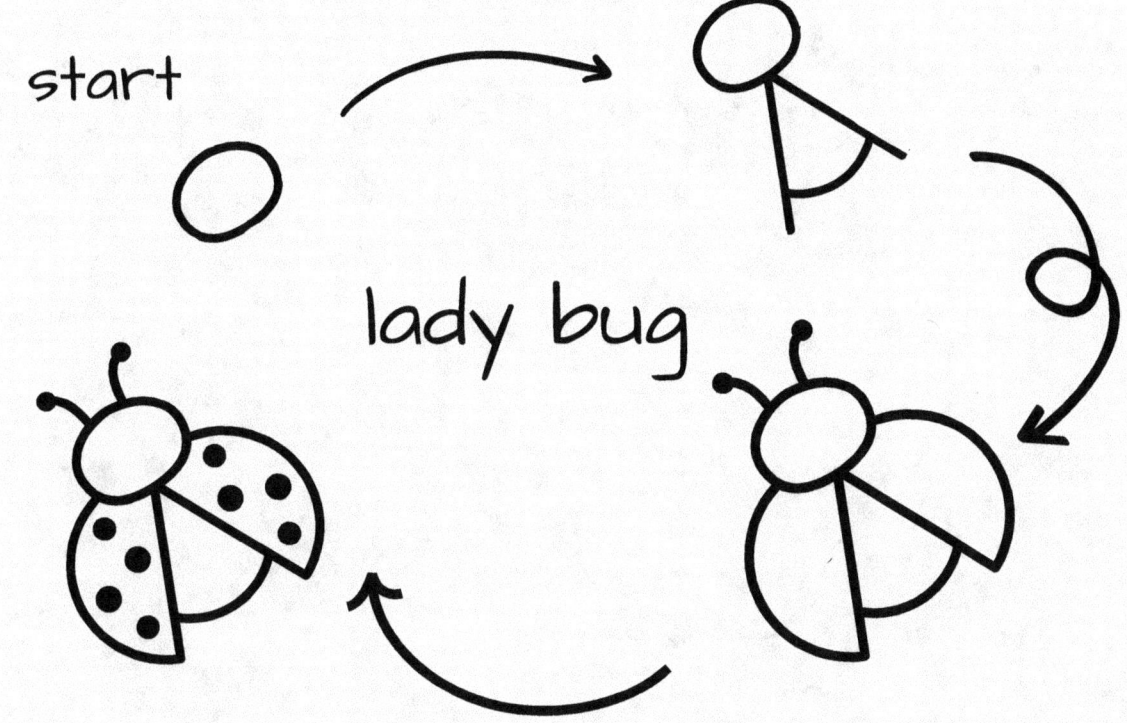

lady bug

your turn

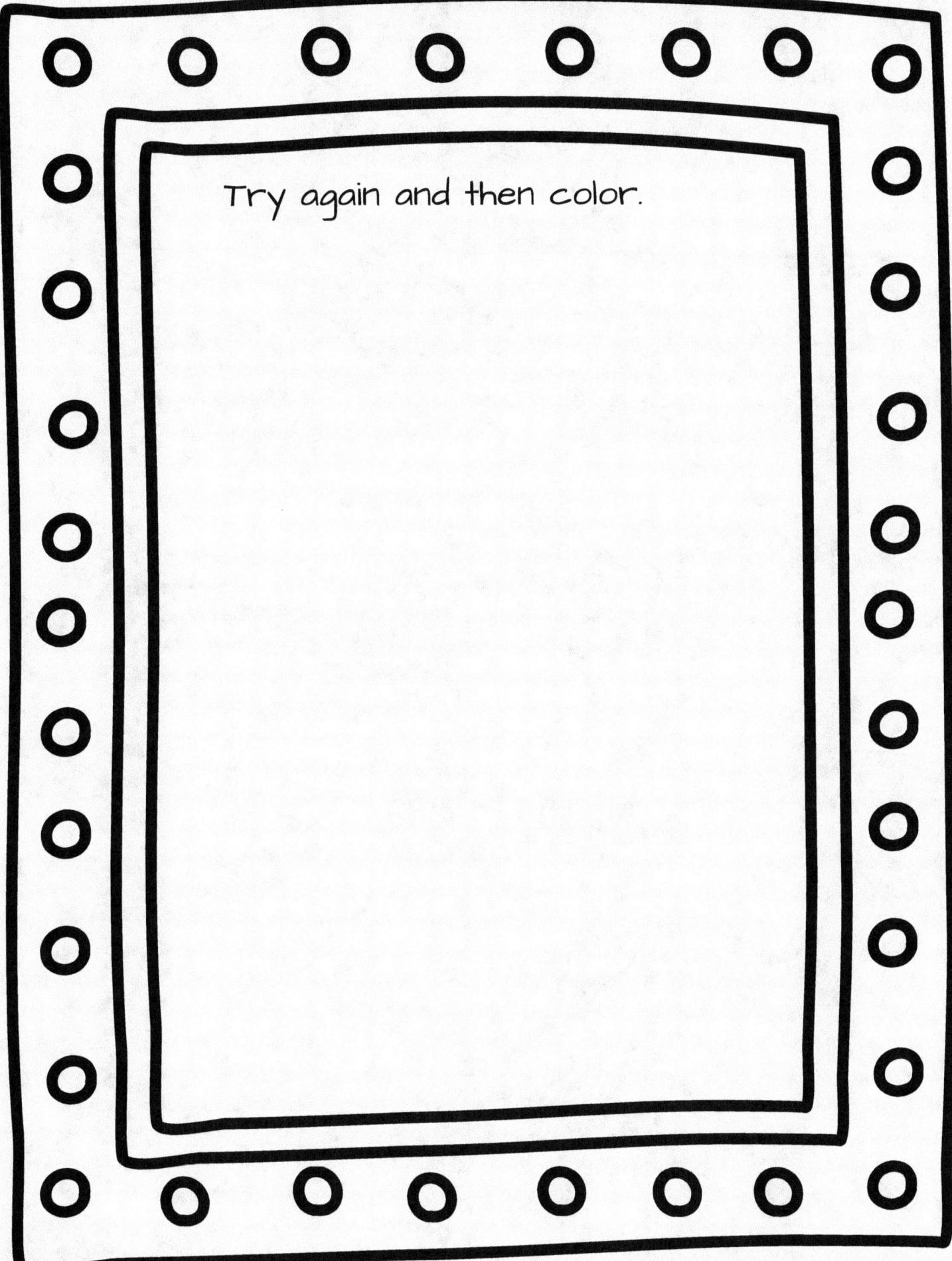
Try again and then color.

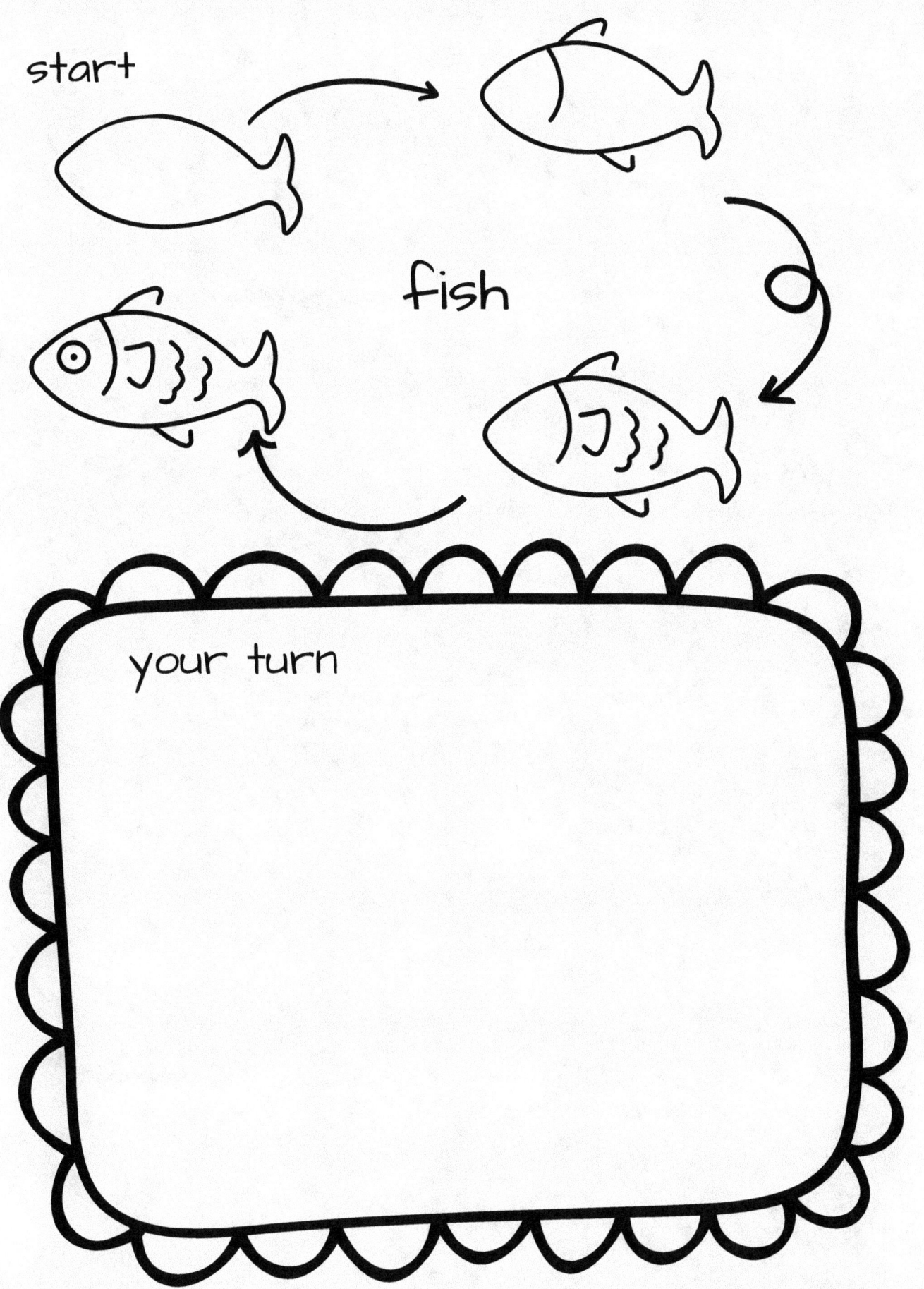

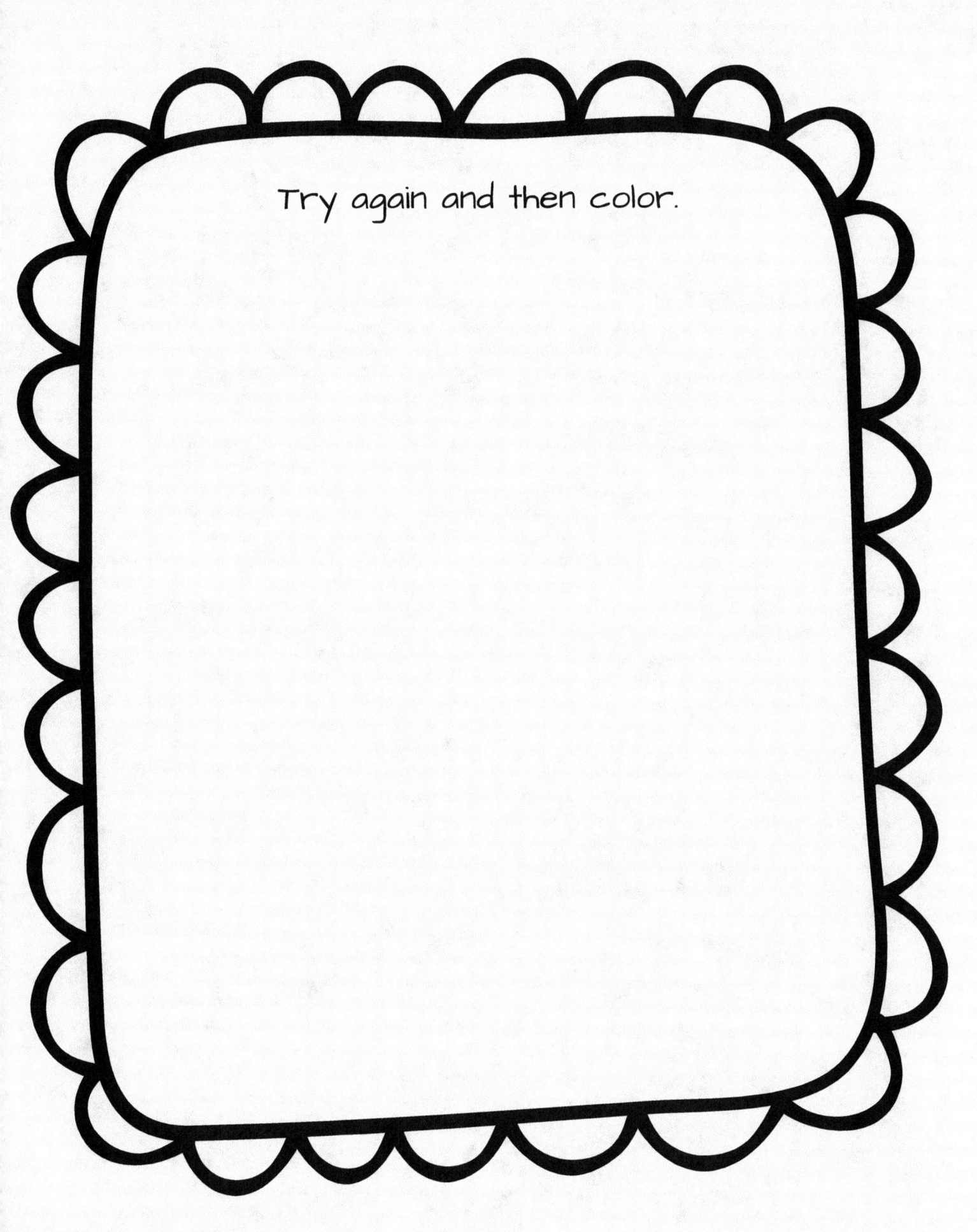
Try again and then color.

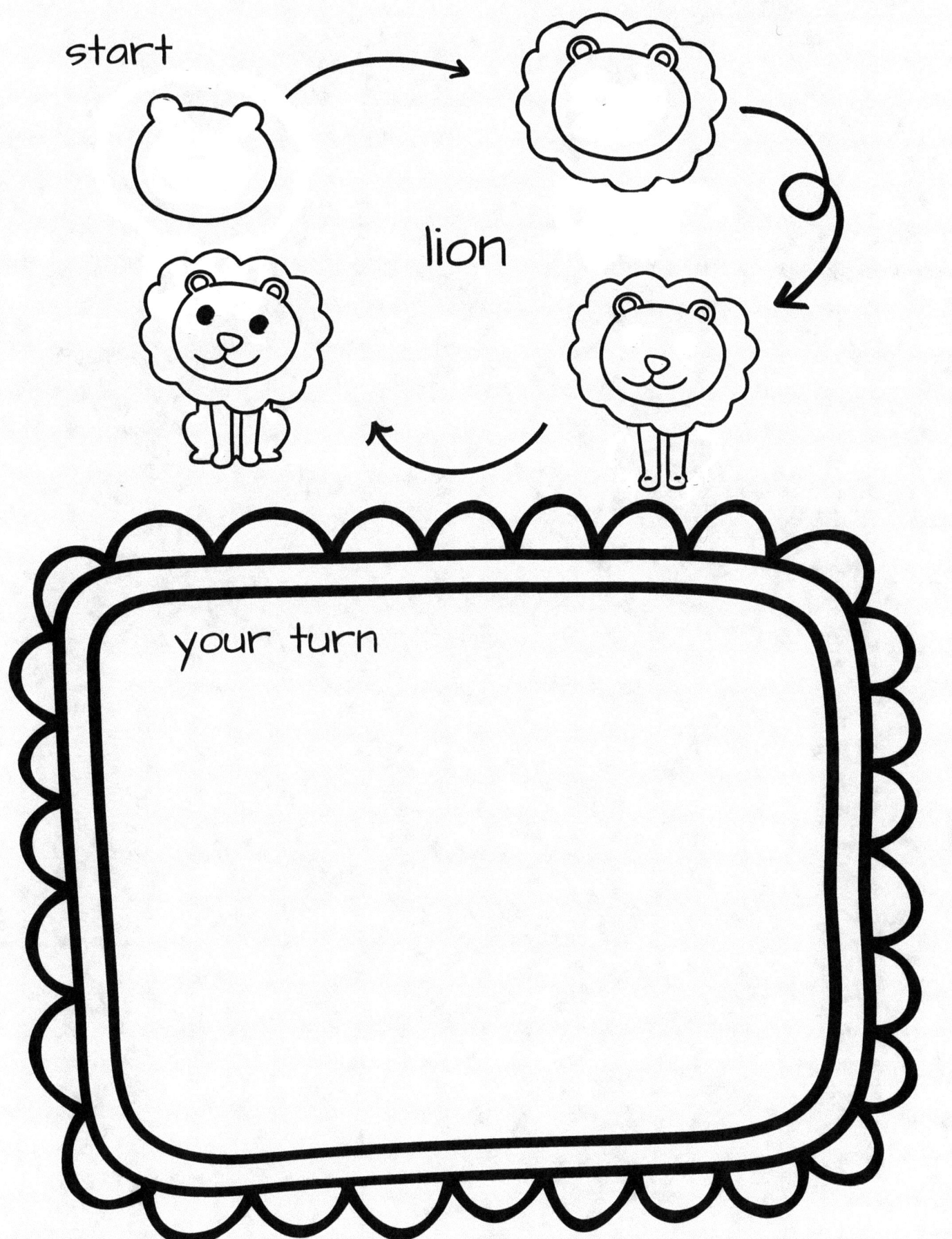

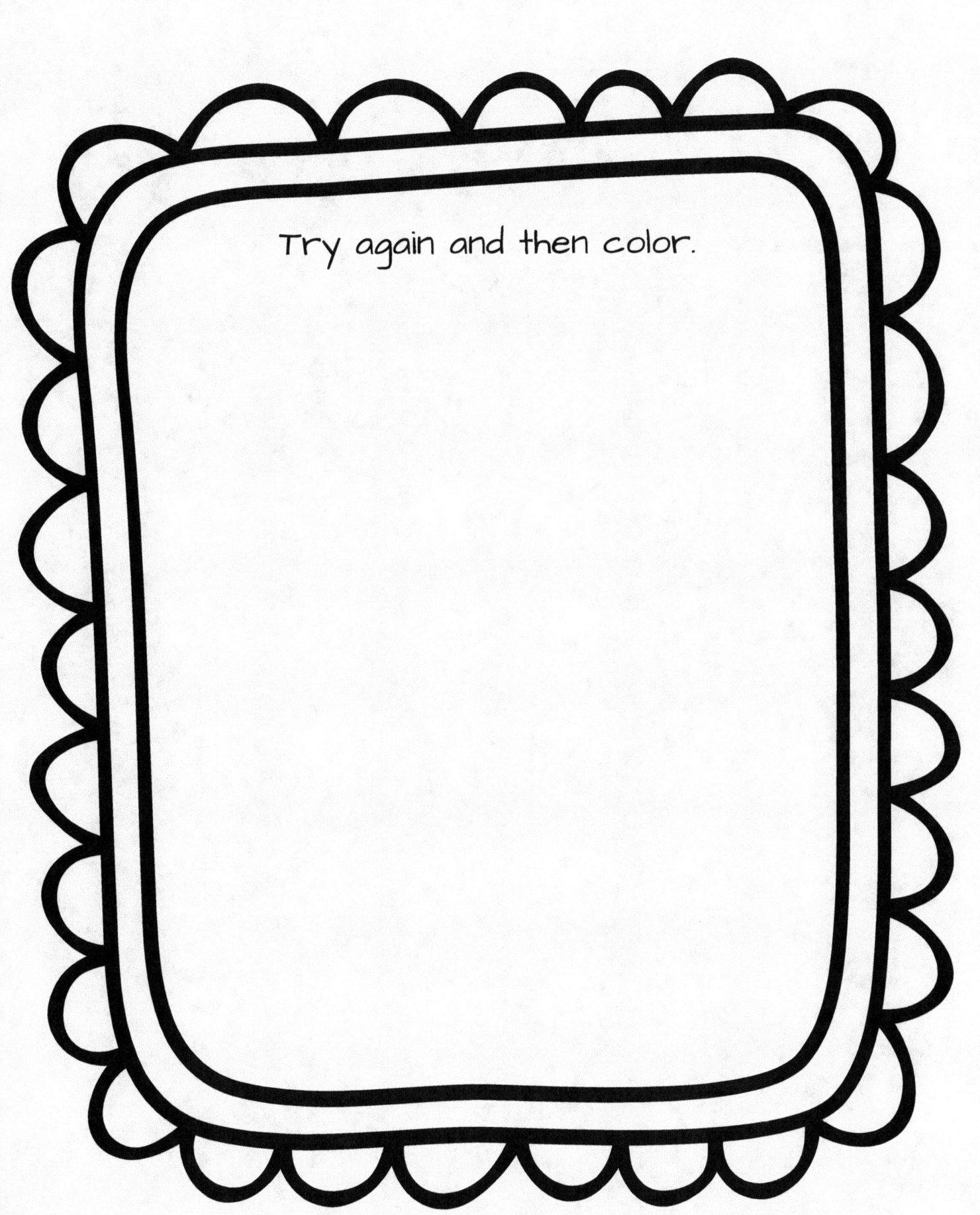
Try again and then color.

start

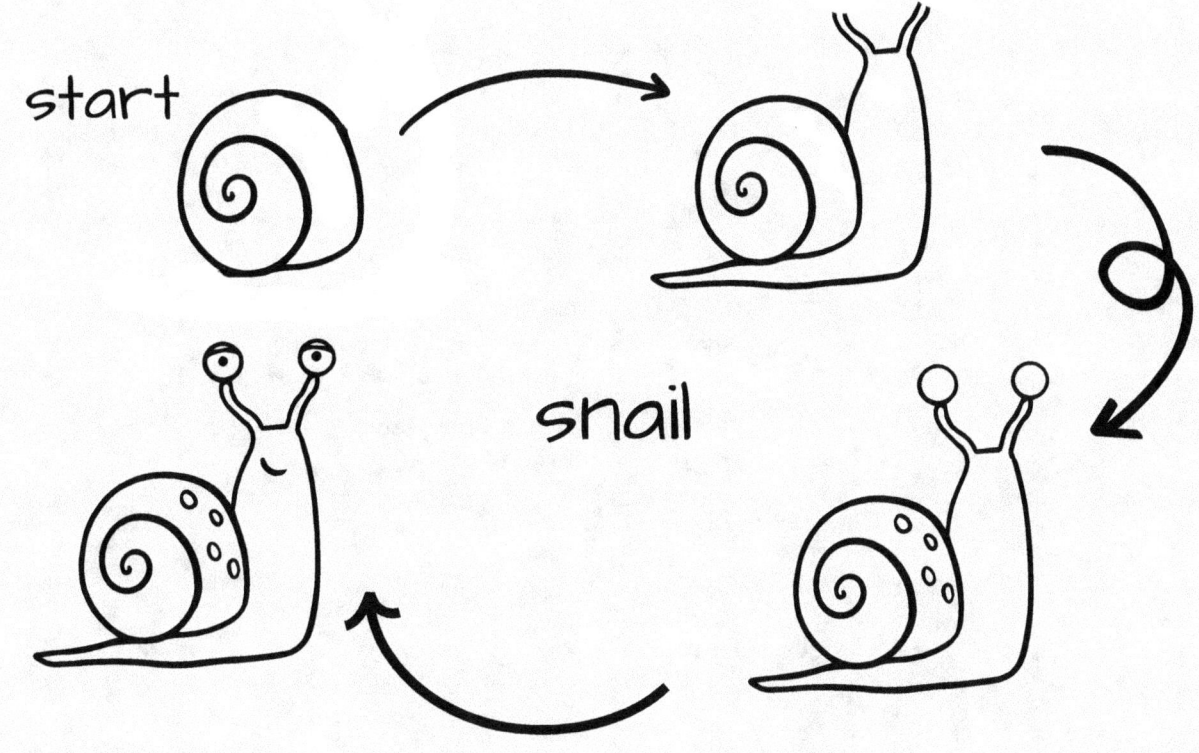

snail

your turn

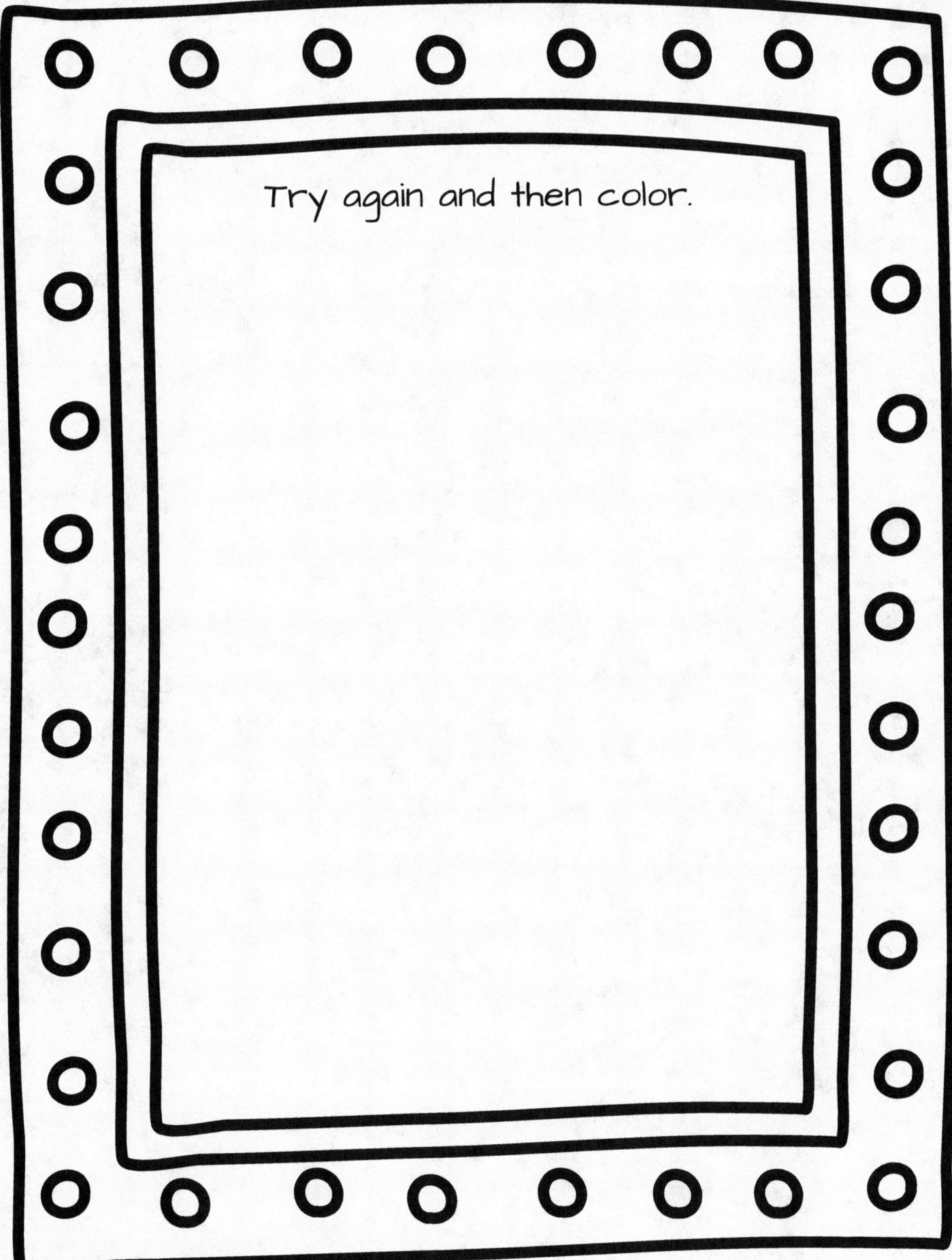
Try again and then color.

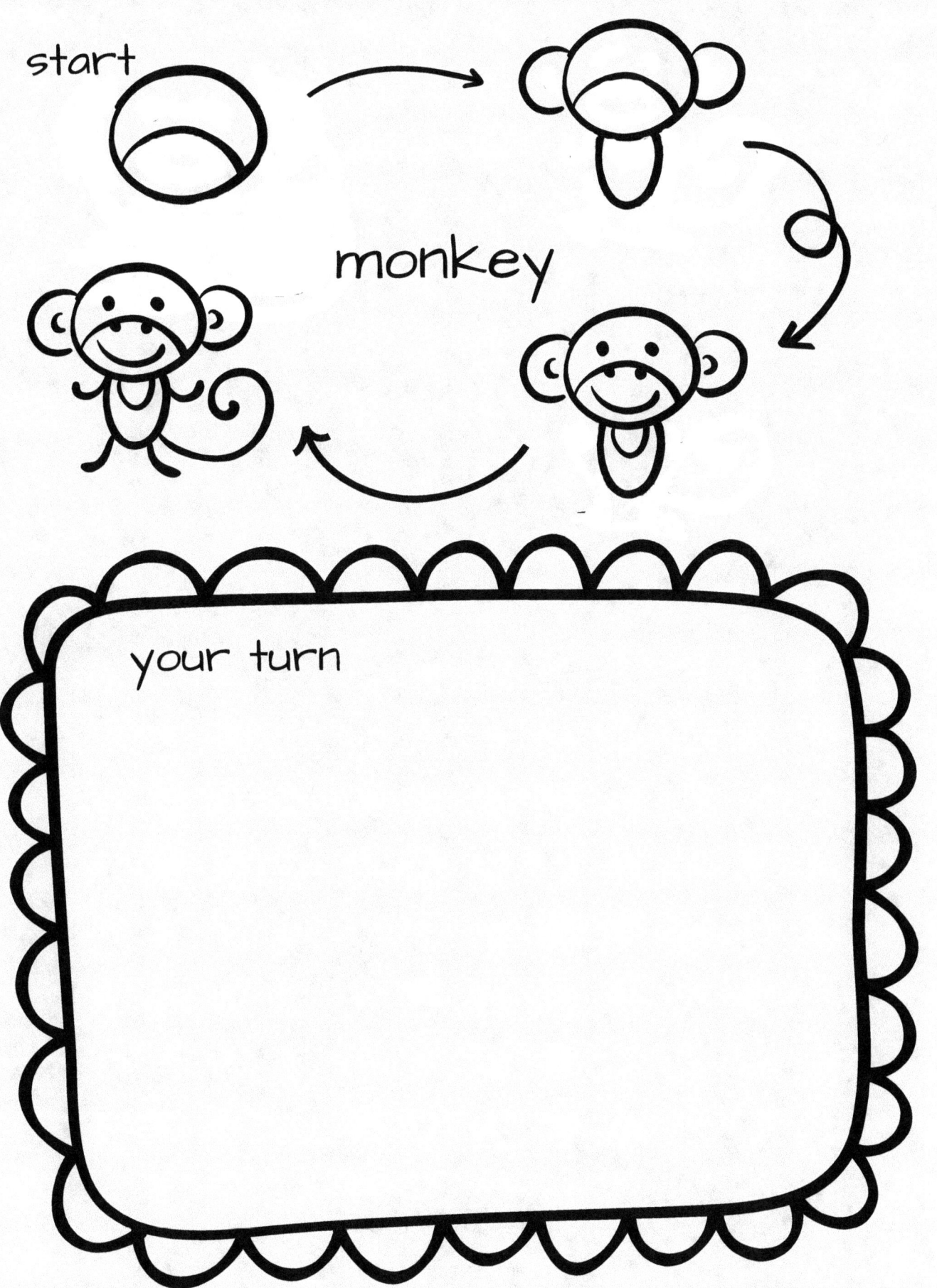

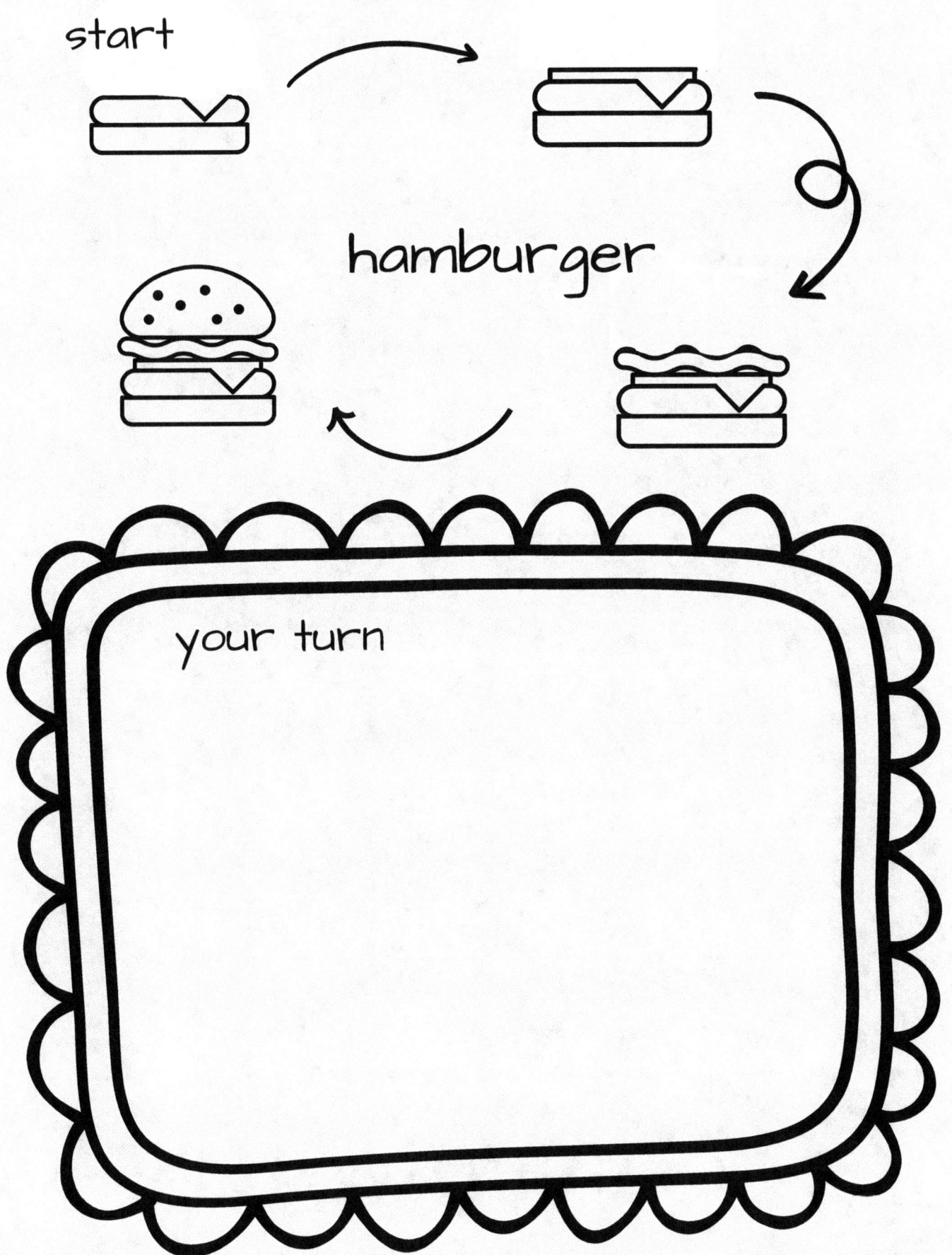

Try again and then color.

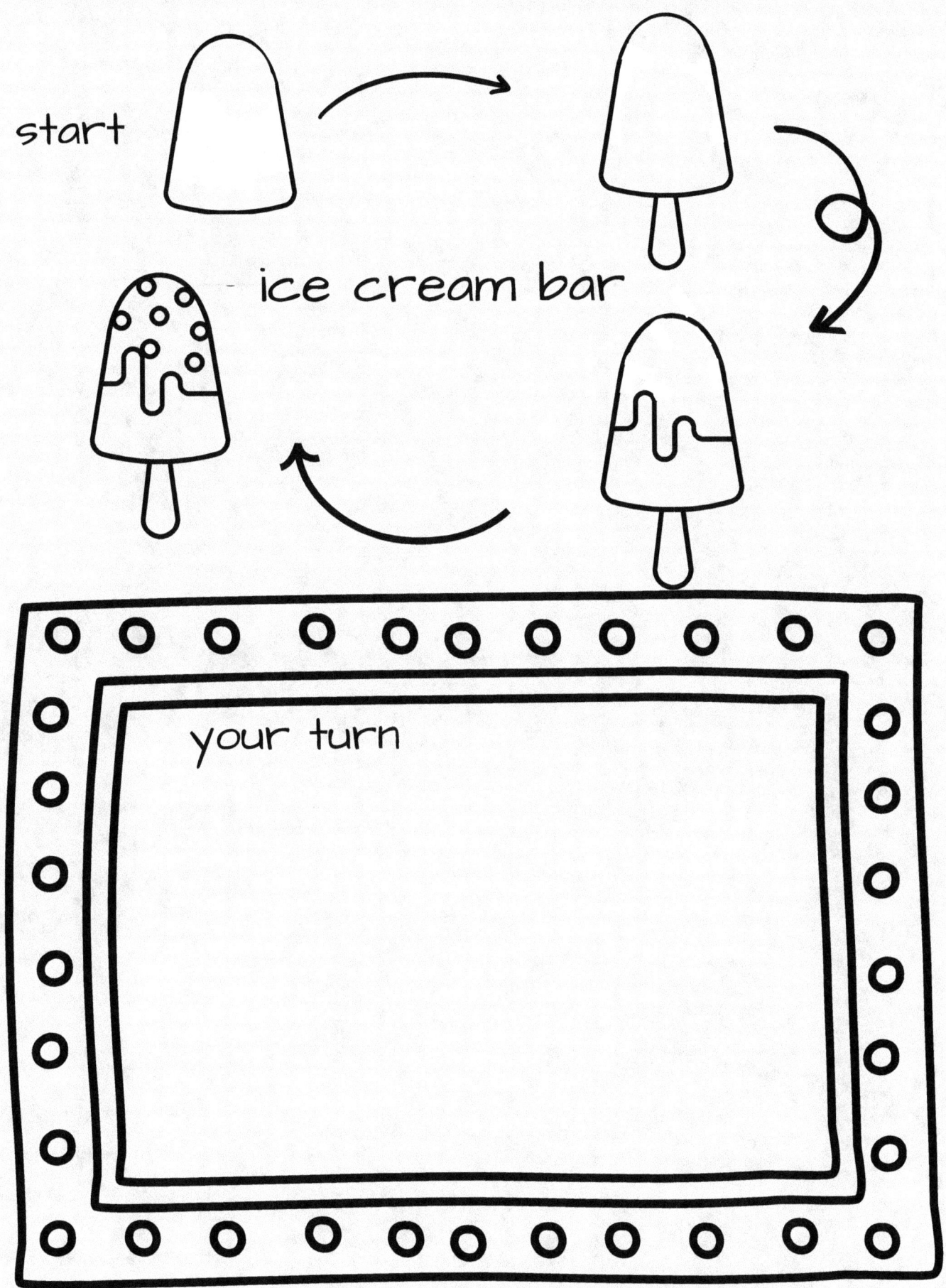

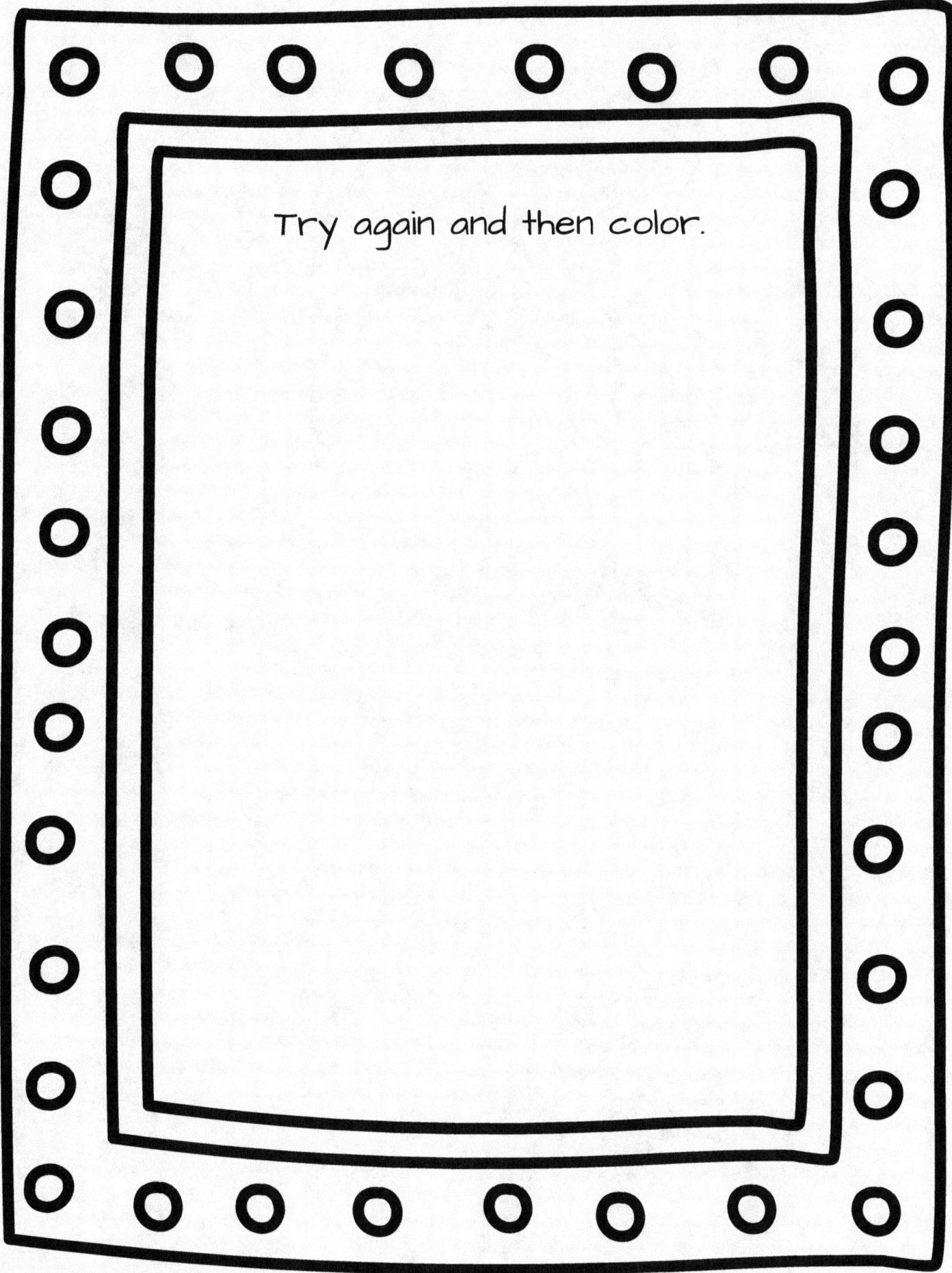
Try again and then color.

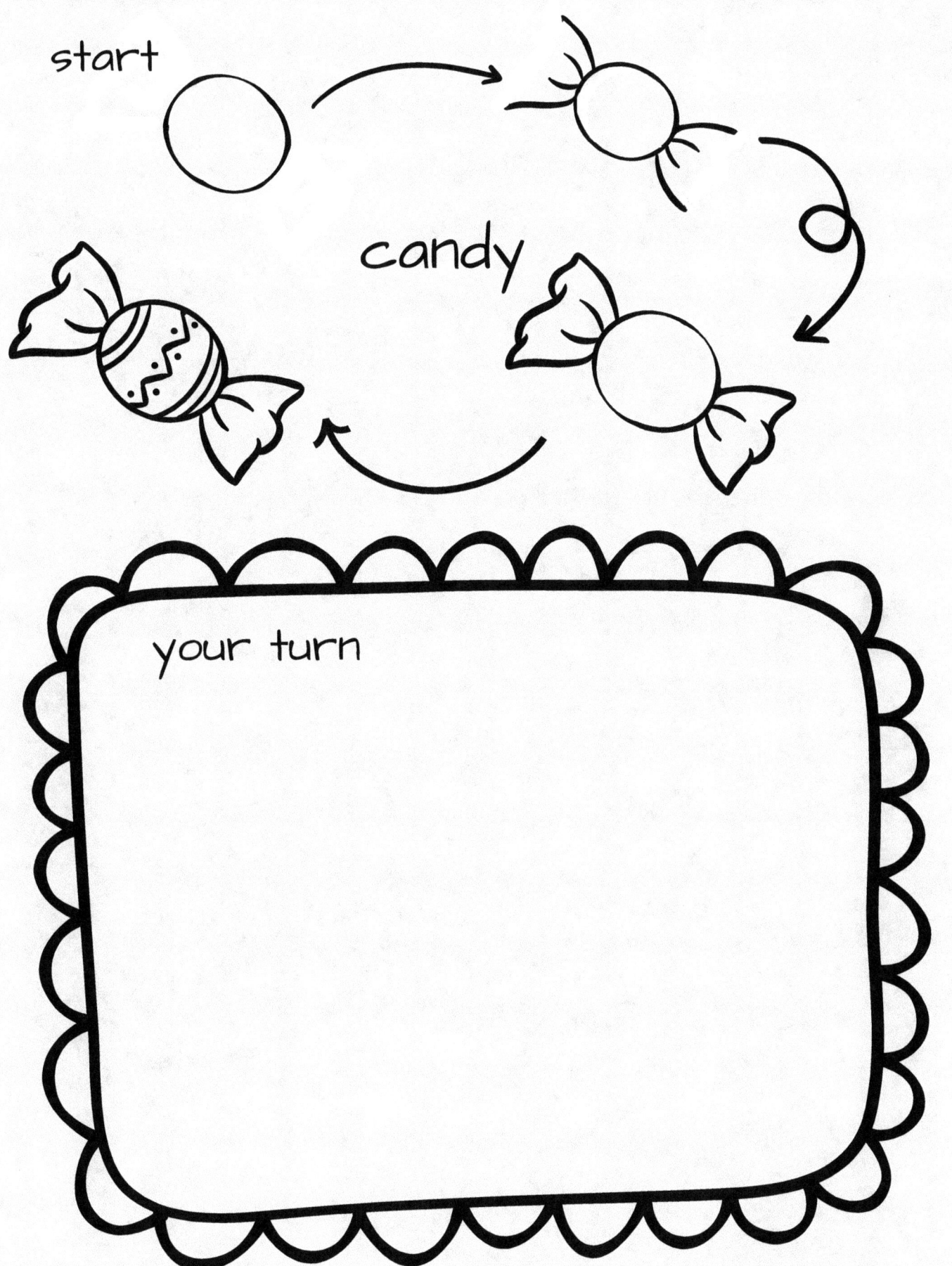

Try again and then color.

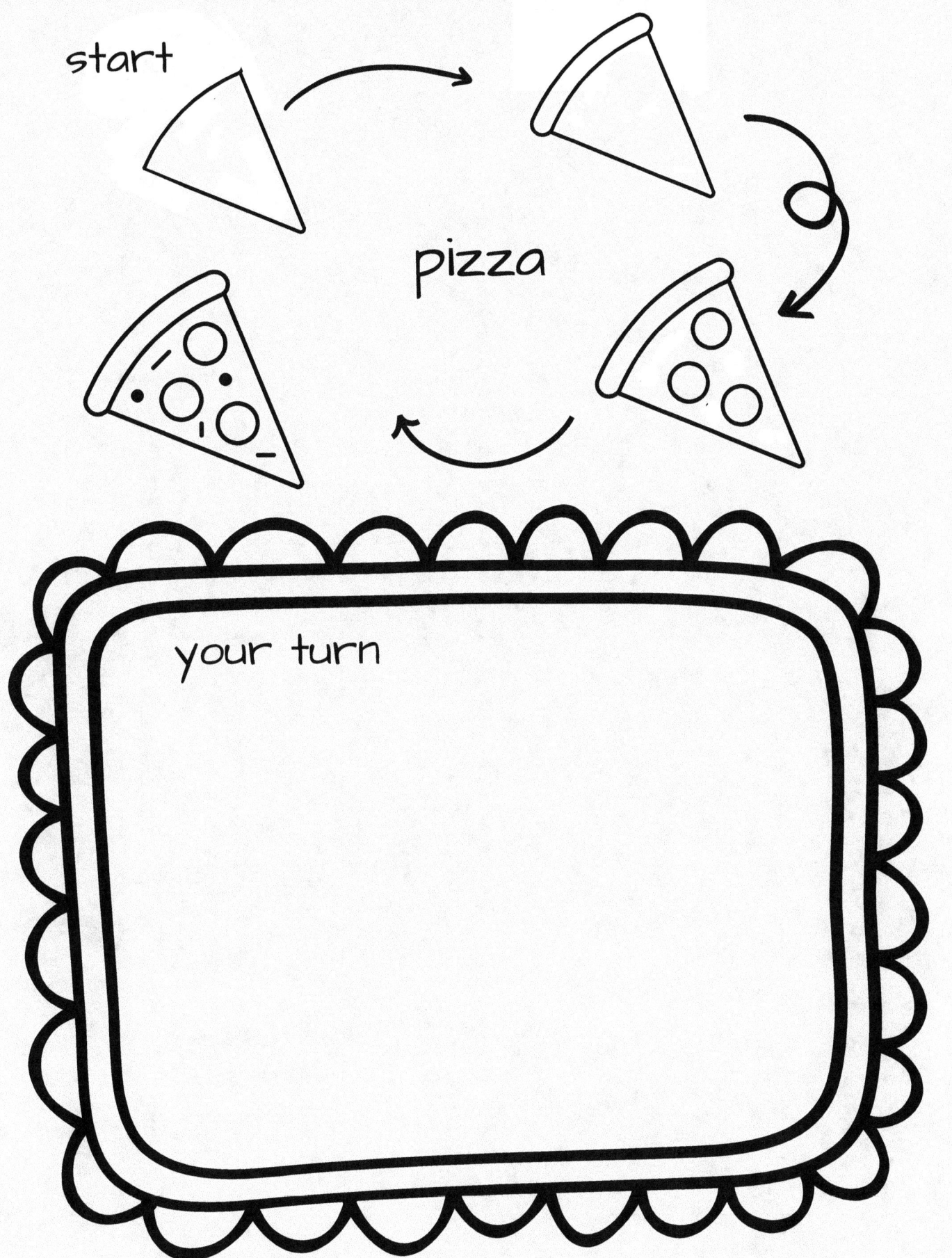

Try again and then color.

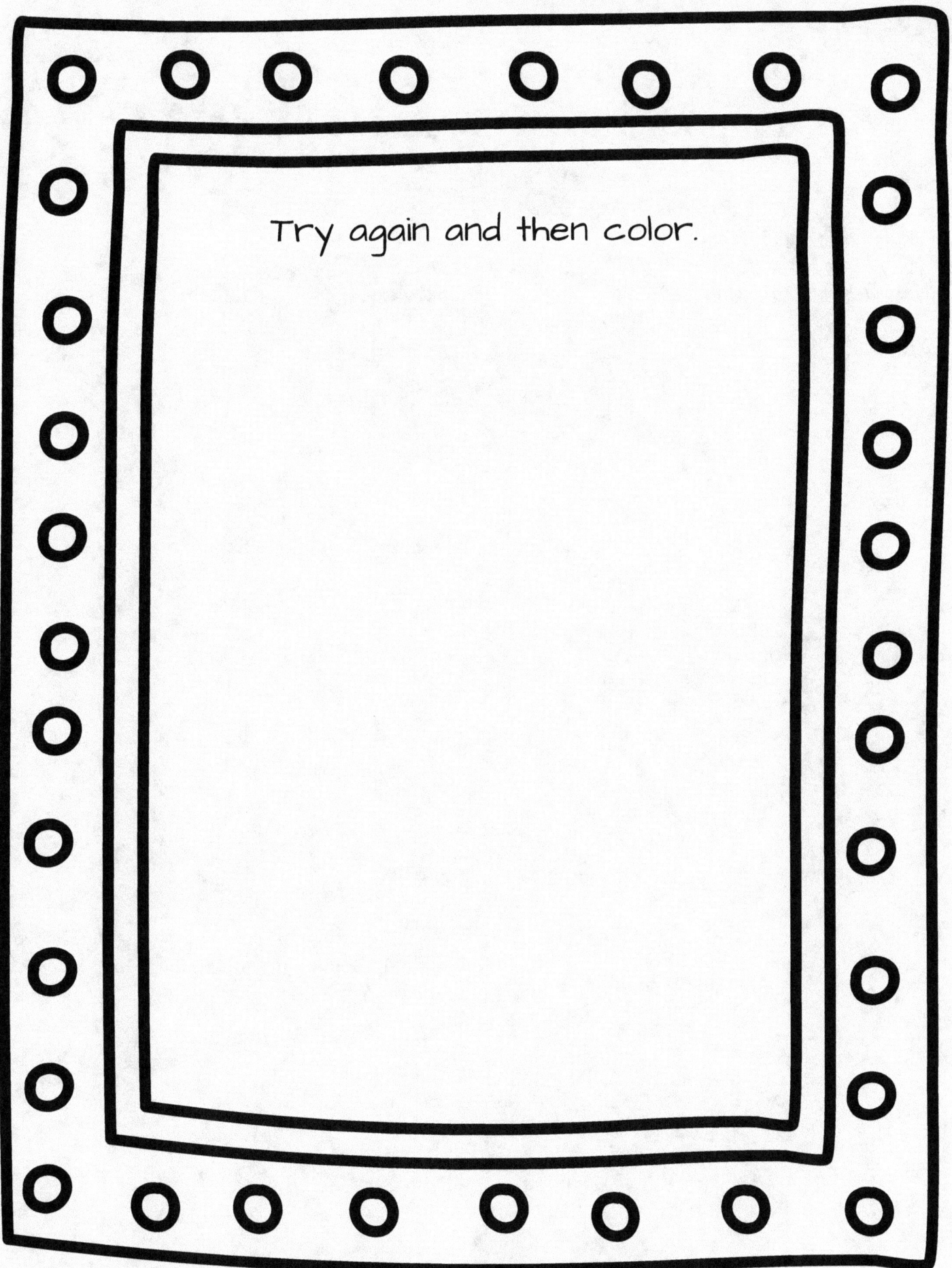
Try again and then color.

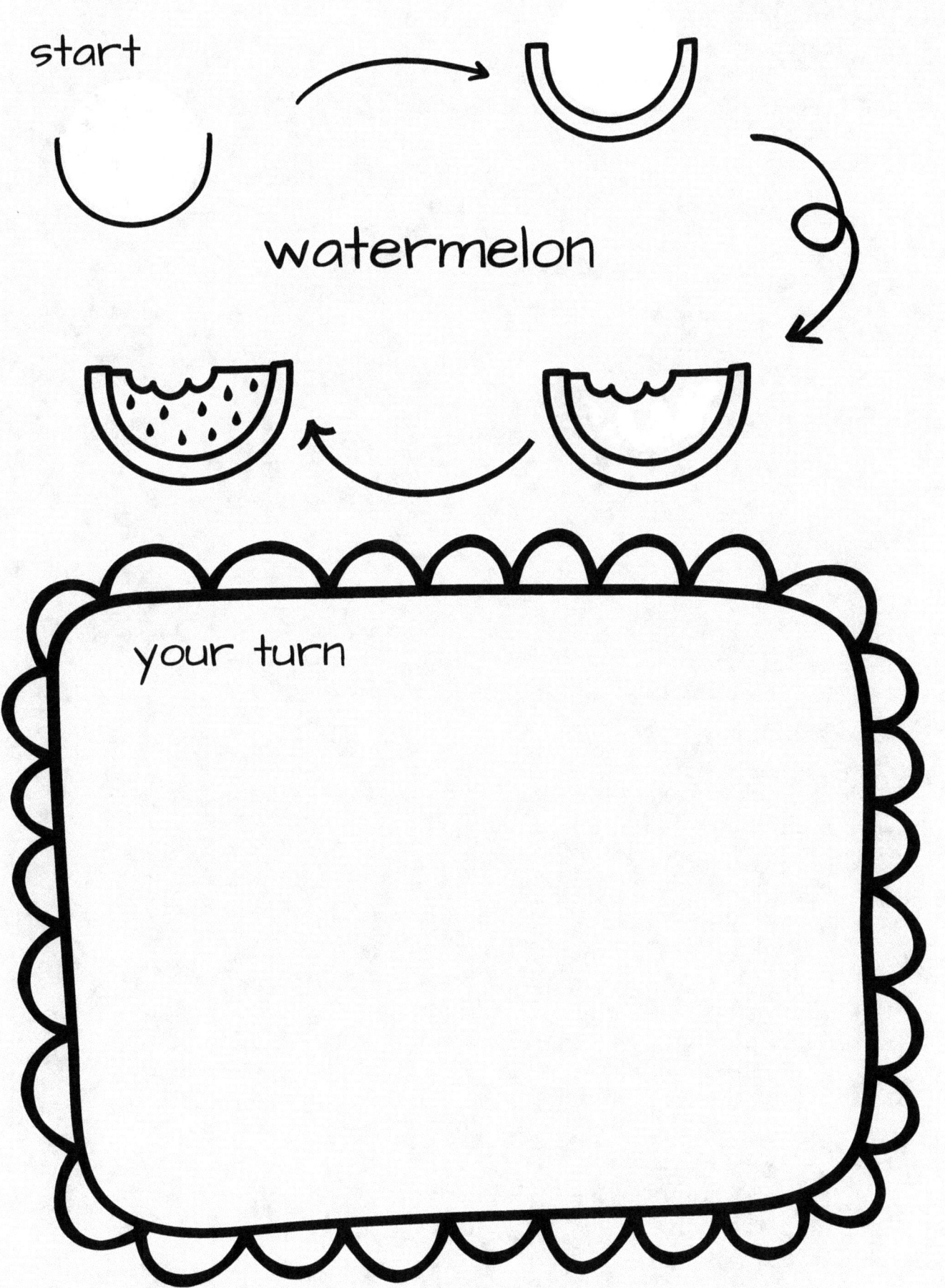

Try again and then color.

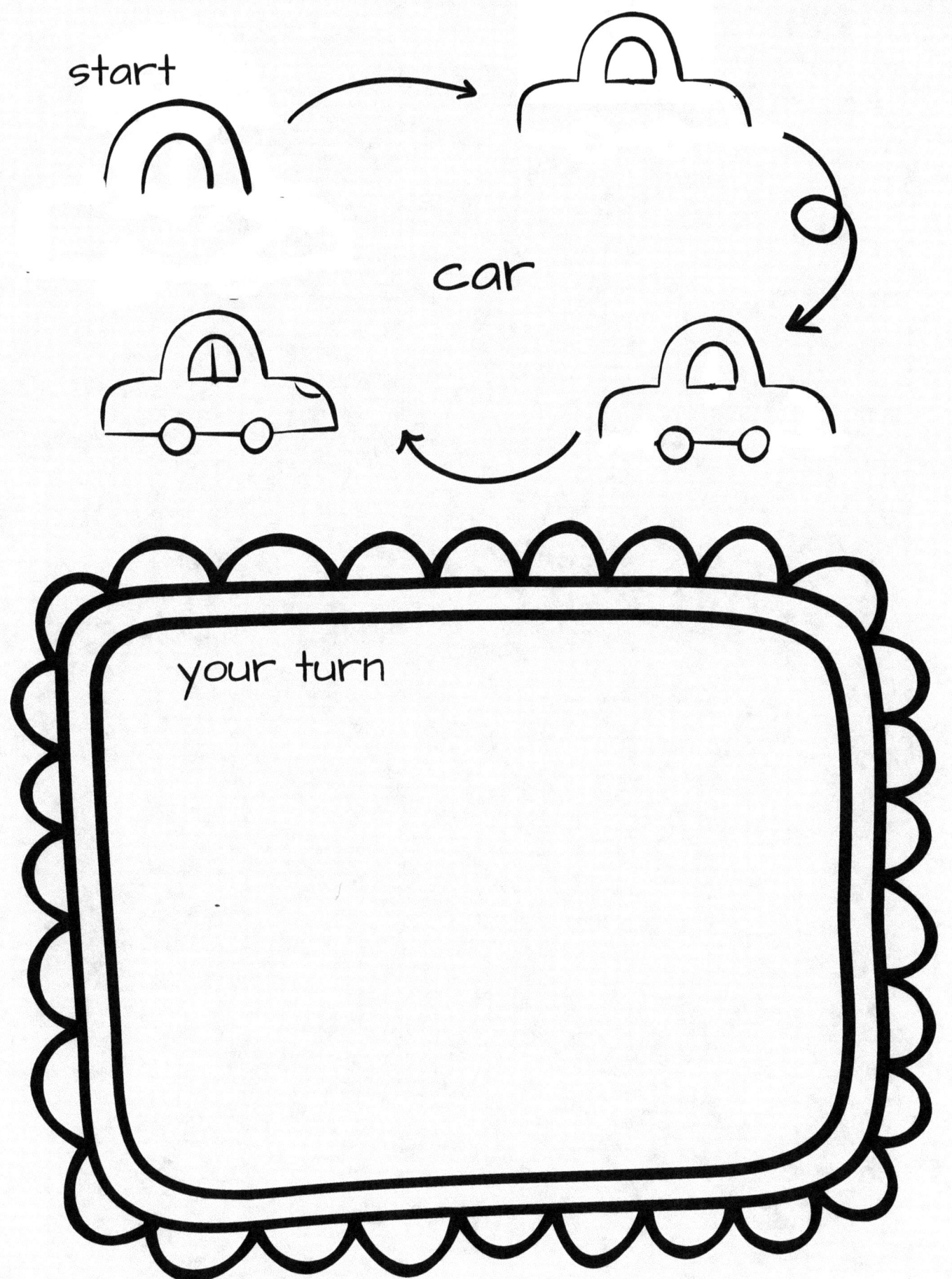

Try again and then color.

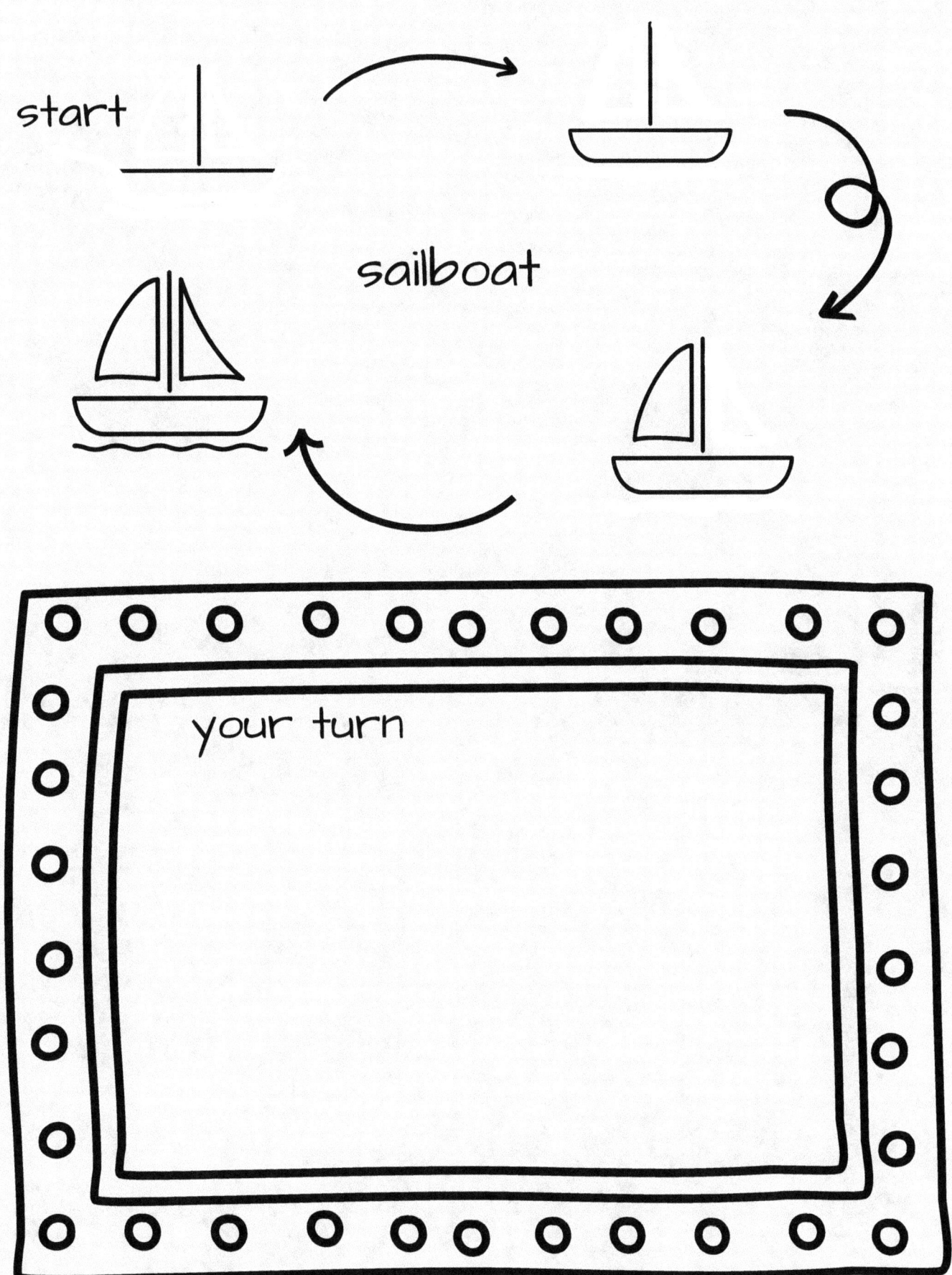

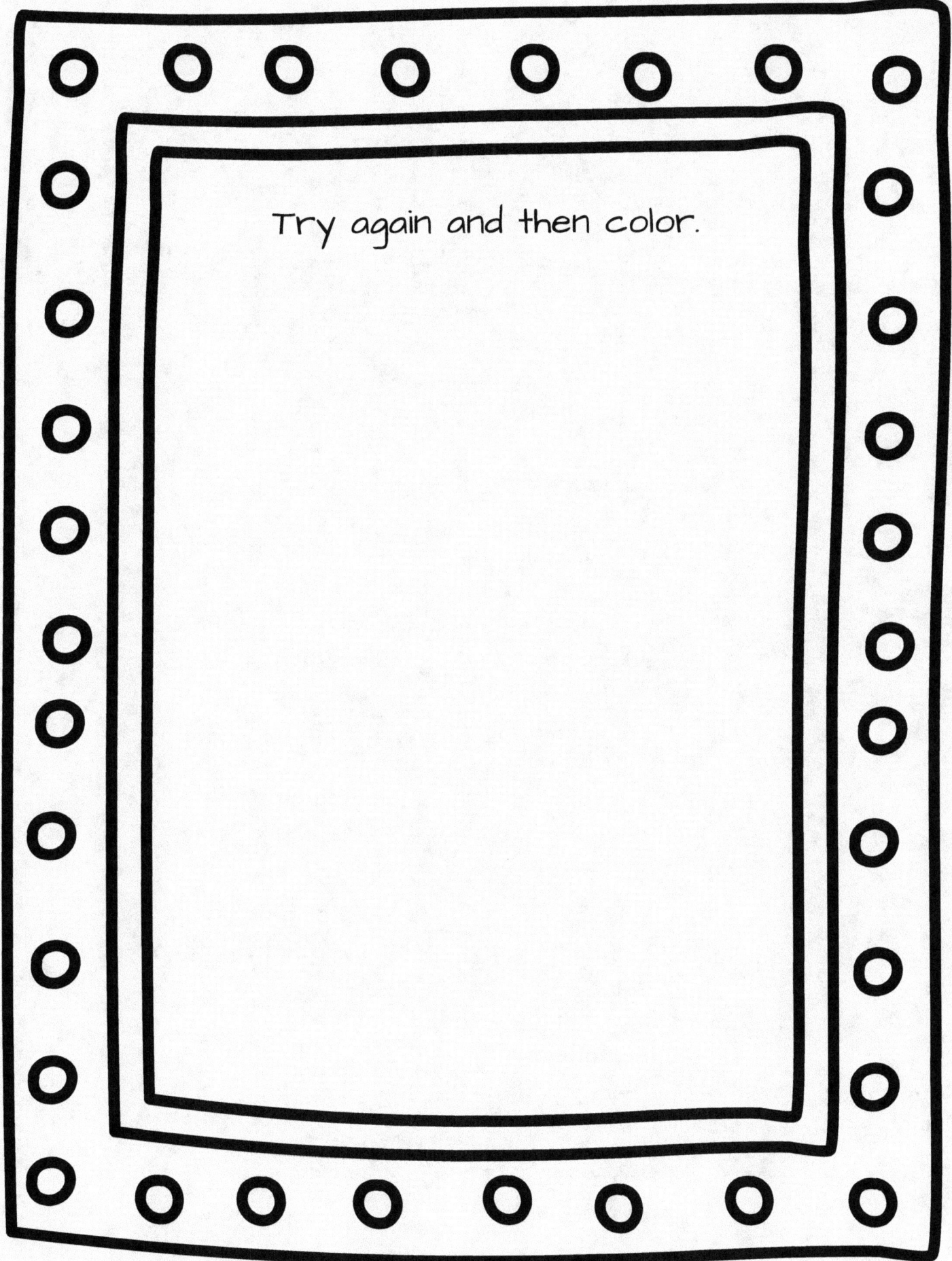
Try again and then color.

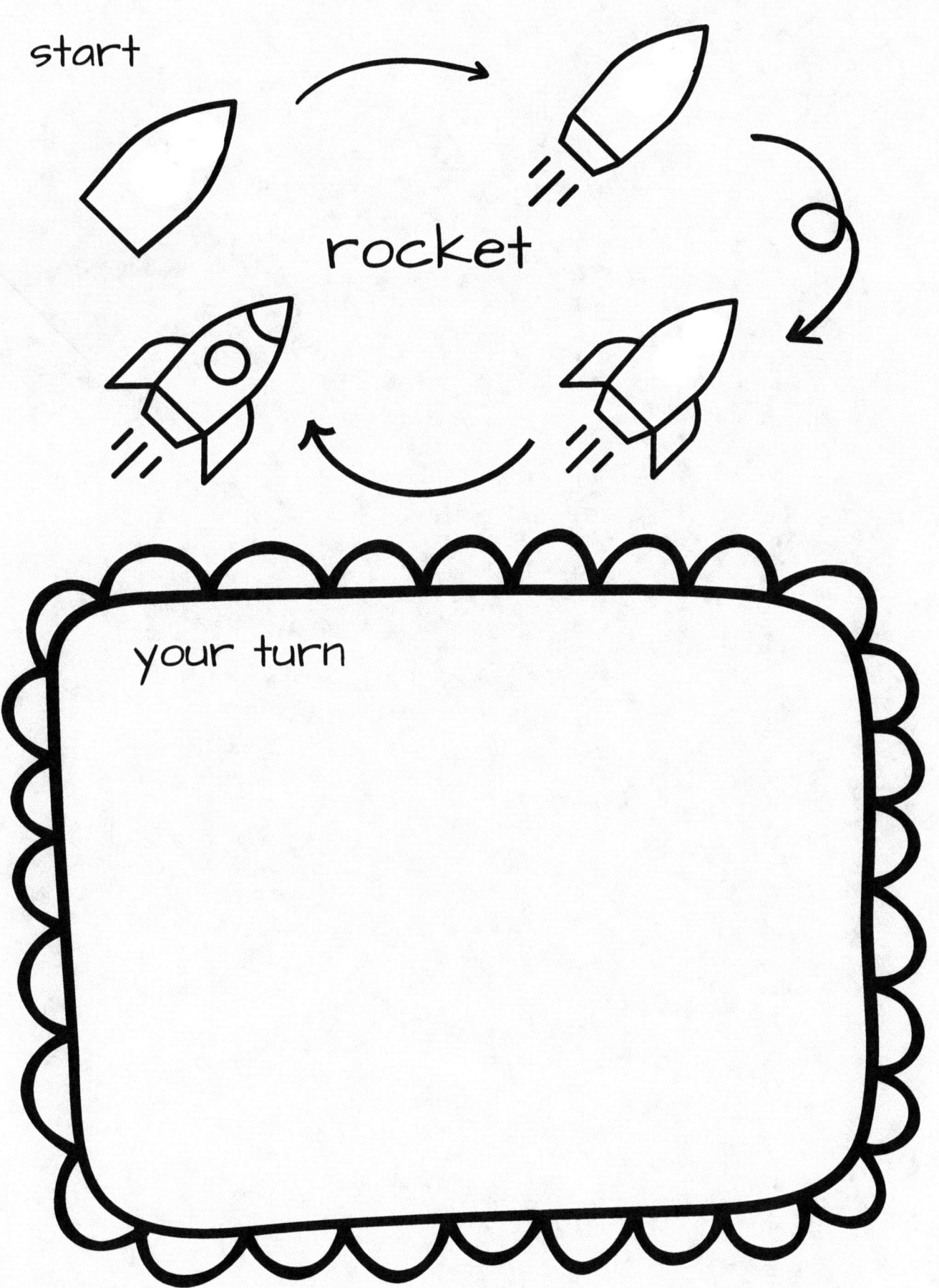

Try again and then color.

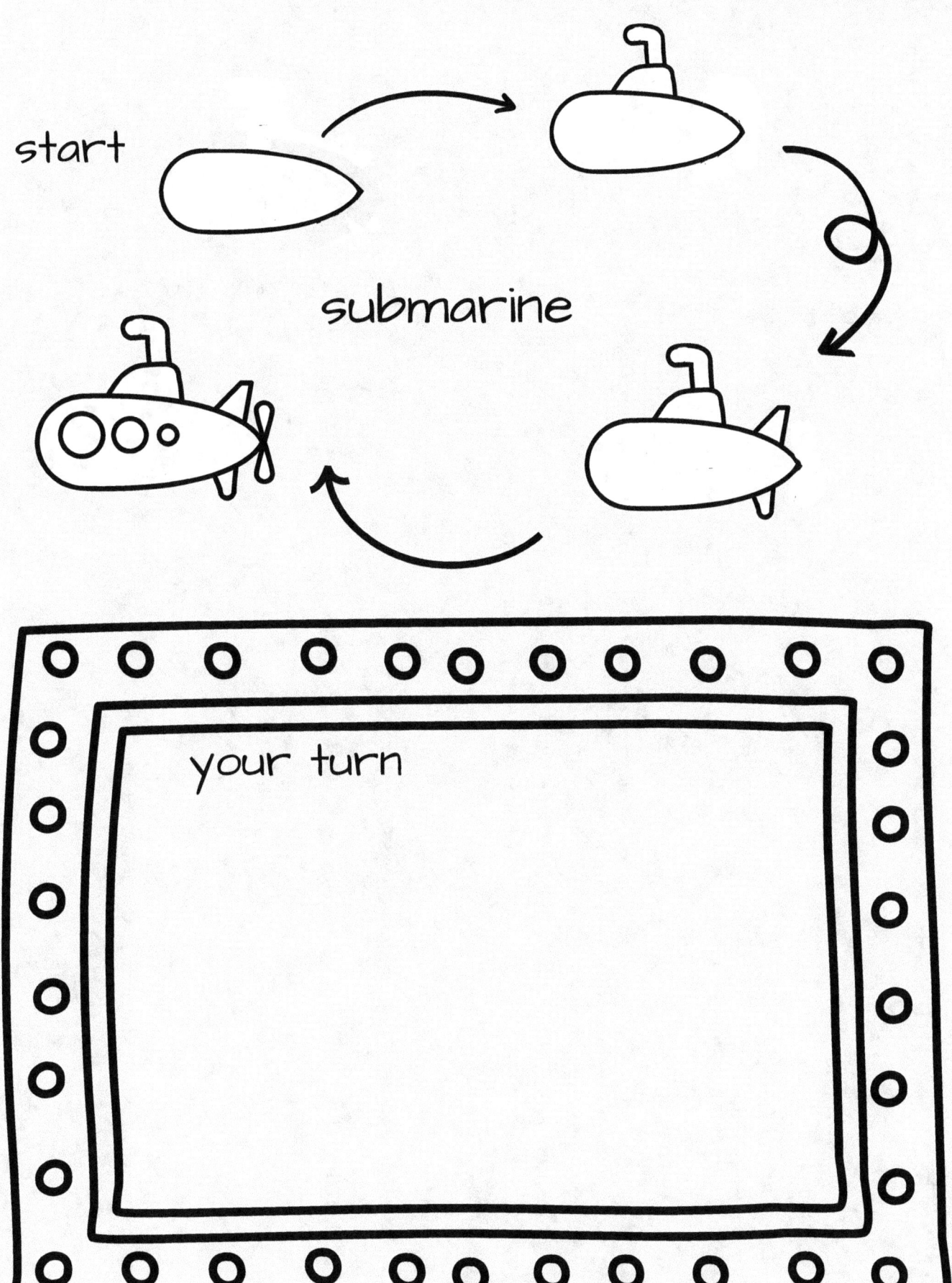

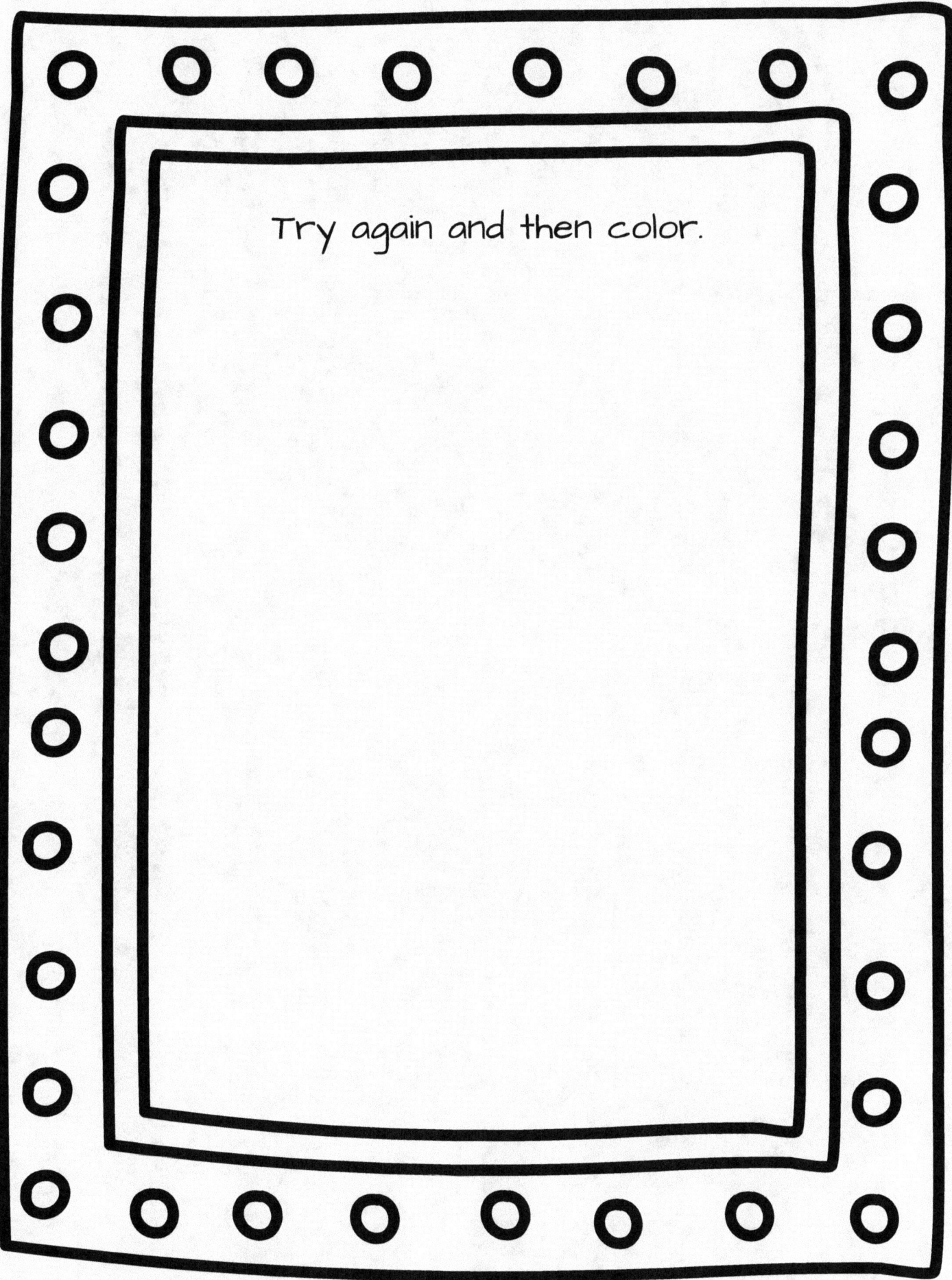
Try again and then color.

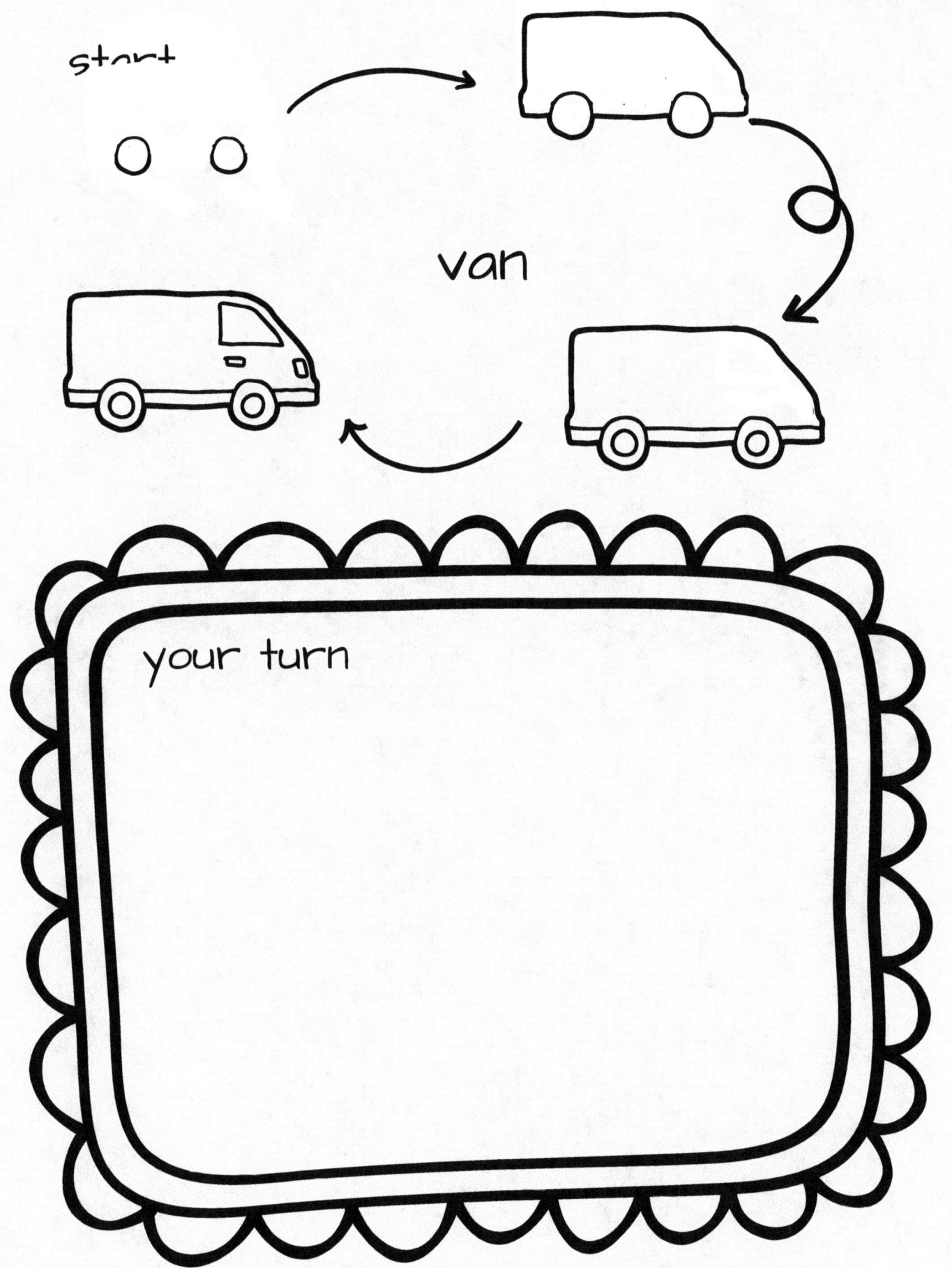

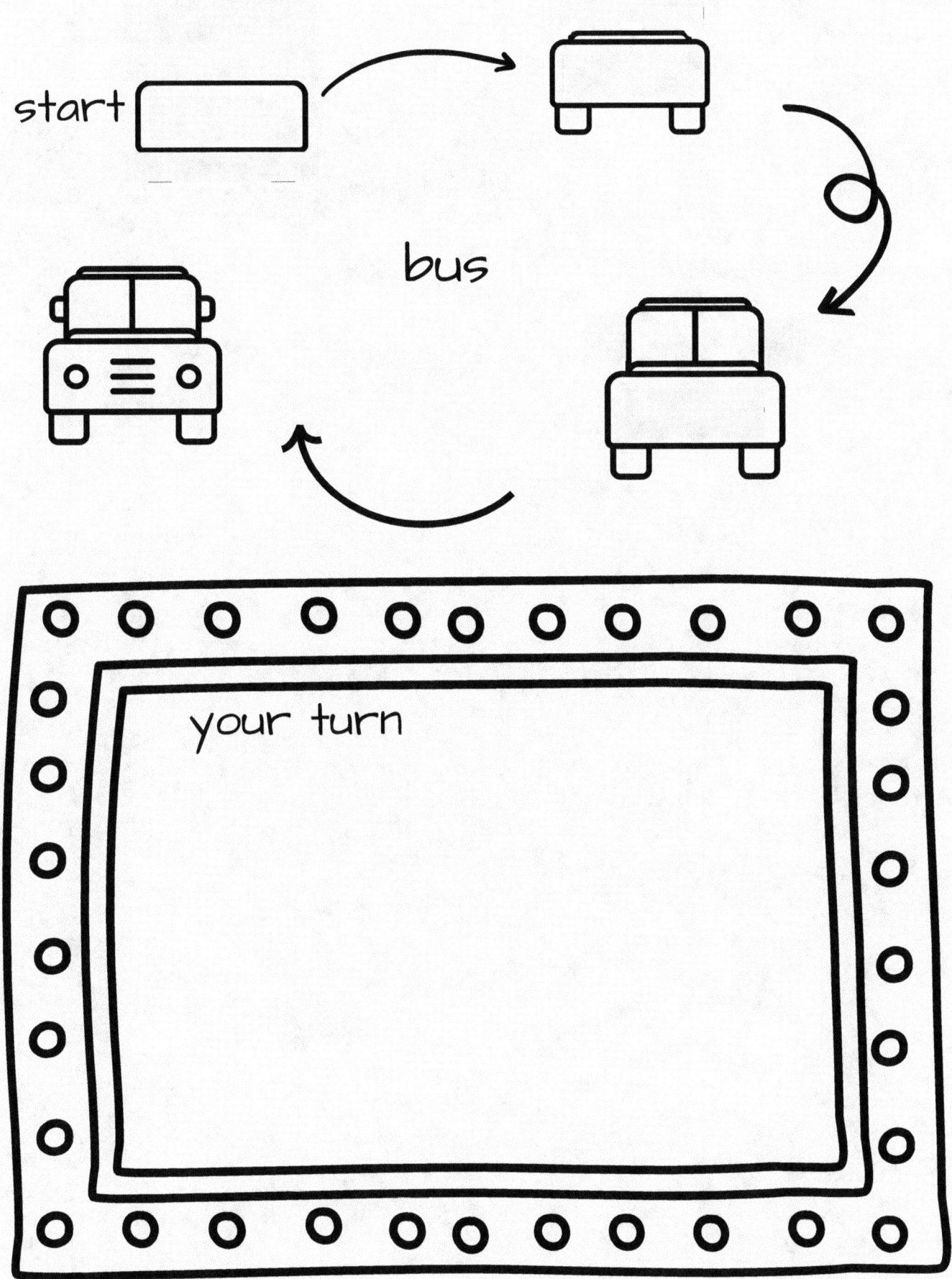

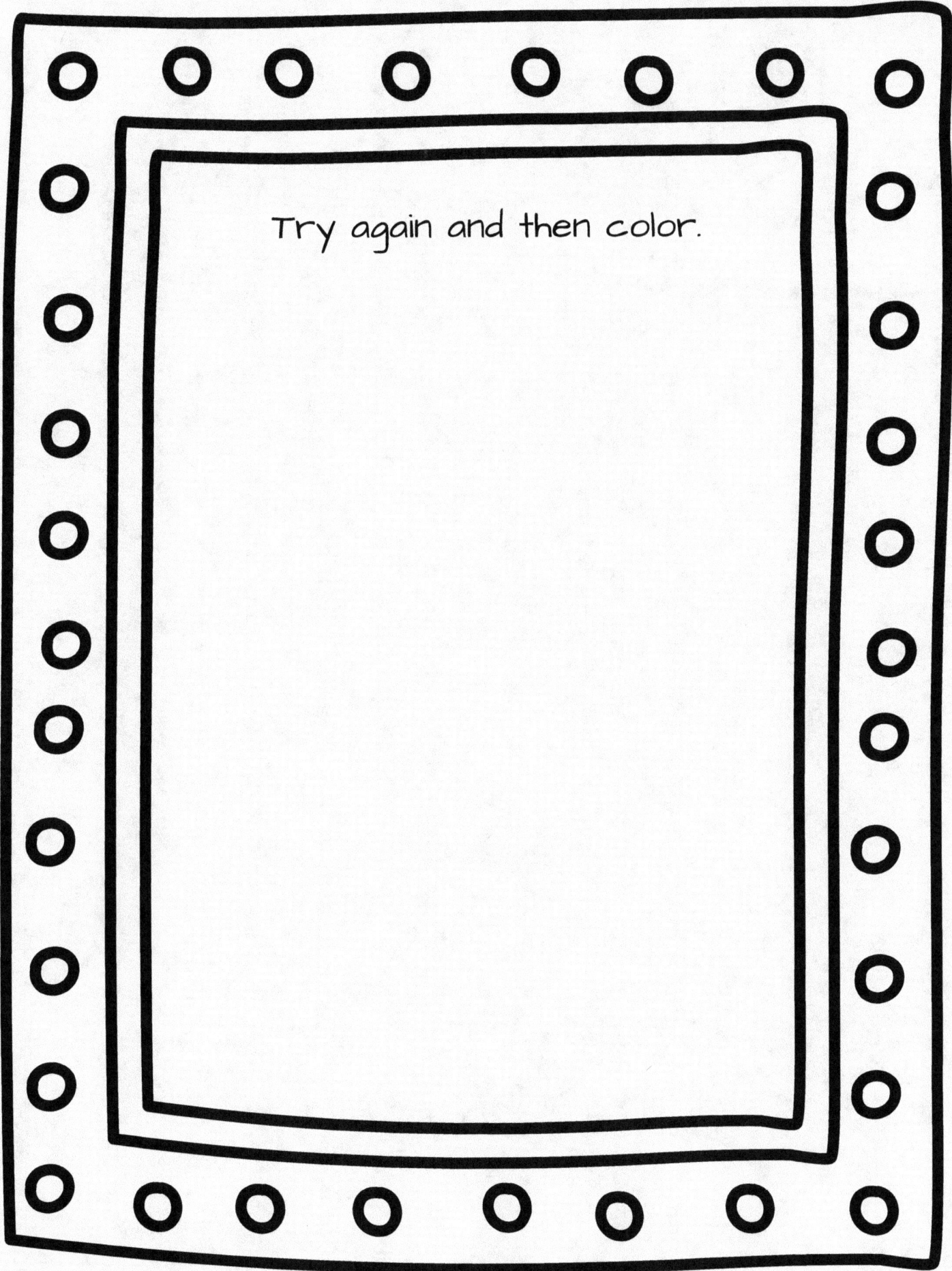
Try again and then color.

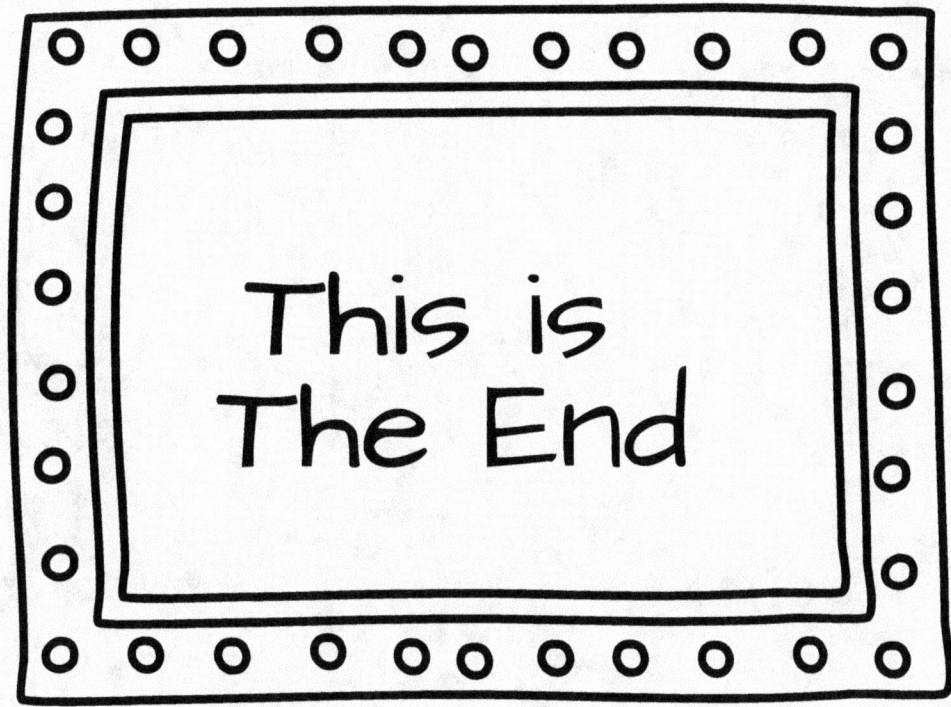

This is The End

I hope you enjoyed this book!
If you did, please leave a kind review on Amazon so other kids can find it.
THanks :)

Here are some more books by
Ms. Josephine's Papers you may like...

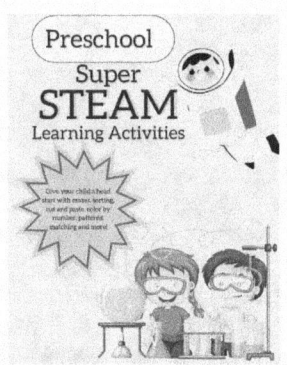
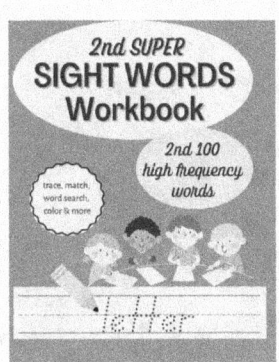
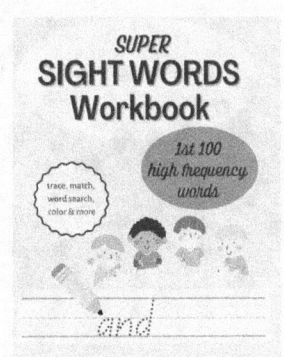
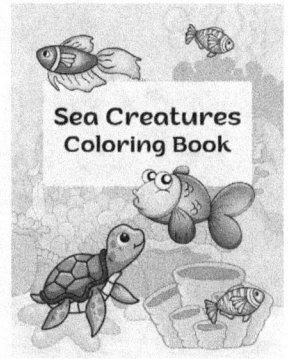

www.ingramcontent.com/pod-product-compliance
Lightning Source LLC
Chambersburg PA
CBHW060436220526
45465CB00008B/3158